A Snowball in Summer

A Snowball
in Summer

Lorn Macintyre

ARGYLL✤PUBLISHING

© Lorn Macintyre 2009

First published 2009

Argyll Publishing
Glendaruel
Argyll PA22 3AE
Scotland
www.argyllpublishing.com

The author has asserted his moral rights.

**British Library Cataloguing-in-Publication
Data.**
**A catalogue record for this book is available
from the British Library.**

ISBN 978 1 906134 30 3

Printing
Athenaeum Press, Gateshead

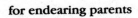
for endearing parents

Contents

Dan Neil MacColl

I no longer need to put up my hand to address you
sitting at your desk, correcting our compositions,
a natty dresser, tweed jacket, tie, shining shoes.
This was long before classroom computers.
The pencil sharpener was screwed to the sill,
beside jars of frog-spawn and crocus bowls.
Under the sloped lid of the desk the tawse,
coiled like a dark serpent with three fangs.
When you used it, it was for breaking strict laws
about not crossing into the girls' shed.
In those post-war years, you had the vision
to make lessons exciting. This afternoon
at handicrafts we are making a fireside brush,
a foot of plaited rope, its end combed out.
We bind it with coloured raffia which hangs
beside your desk like the mane of an exotic
creature. You chalked the Gaelic songs
on the blackboard for us to sing.
On summer afternoons, you took the classes
across the quiet road, up into Achaleven,
lying on the grass to identify the flowers.
I can still spot the lesser celandine.
One winter morning you were absent.
A few days later, I stood with the senior class
lining the road down from St Oran's Church.
As your coffin passed, my knees were knocking,
but not from the cold of that December day.
Last night I called up your death certificate
on my computer: *coronary artery thrombosis*.
I thought of you and my heart gave a lurch.

Accumulator

The glass accumulator I carried home,
acid slopping round its cells
perilously close to bare legs
contained dance bands, Gaelic choirs.

You had to scrape the terminals
with a match box before connecting
to the wireless with its gold mesh
standing on the sill like an icon.

Through its glowing valves
I heard Churchill's exhortations,
Aunt Kathleen on Children's Hour,
the first broadcasts of the Goons.

We couldn't get the Third Programme
because of the mountains
shutting us into a land of Gaelic songs,
not the symphonies of Brahms.

When *Allt an Dubh*, the dark stream,
was reduced to a trickle, time
to carry the accumulator
back to the electrician's

to be recharged with a culture
that was already fading.
When the valves blew
they were irreplaceable.

Egg Thief

You could tell the boy was an egg thief; thin furtive face.
I was going to write: like a fox's, but that's to demean
that elusive creature foraging for survival. This boy
lived in a substantial house in the village, abutted
by a wood where he did most of his hunting.
He wasn't like the tinkers, who had to get by
on gulls' eggs when the peg market was glutted.
He was relentless in his pursuit of nests, and would shin
up trees, crawl into shrubberies. Once, he boasted,
he had swum across to the island on the loch,
put the grebe's egg into his mouth for the return.
One evening he invited me down to his basement
to watch him. He made holes in the ends with a needle,
then gently blew the yellow embryo from the sphere
with a thin glass tube between his thin cruel lips.
The girls' shed was out of bounds. Some of the boys
crossed the wall into the toilet to compare genitals.
When the egg thief went, he unwrapped the cotton wool
to show them his latest acquisition, like a jewel.
Some of the boys said this was how he got a feel.
He kept his collection in a compartmented glass-lidded case.
His greatest treasure was a cuckoo's egg. He was daft,
bringing it to school. When the bully spotted it,
he took it on his palm, studied its greenness, laughed,
then spat in the thief's face as he closed his fist.

Ferreting

Banker by day, father became
a backwoodsman when he shed
stud and collar in the evening.
All he lacked, a racoon cap.

We had guns, rods, a polecat ferret,
wicked-eyed, in champagne coat.
It flowed down my arm,
biting the hand that fed it.

He put a gold ring on its snout
in case it decided to dine out.

We drove in pegs by the burrows,
mesh spread in our fingers,
like mother protecting her perm
with a hair net at bed-time.

I put my ear to the turf,
listening to the thumping heart
of the earth, a rabbit bowling
into the net.

Father took care of it.
I pressed out the stream of piss
with thumbs in the warm fur.
Mother wouldn't skin it.

One night the ferret didn't emerge.
Stripped to his semmit, father threw
shovelfuls at the risen moon.
At one a.m. he uncovered the miscreant,

curled up, asleep, with a weight problem.

Thermogene

When the first cold spell of winter came
my father donned his golden breastplate.
It wasn't like St Patrick's *lorica*, to protect
him against the arrows of a host of demons,
assuring him immediate entry at heaven's gate.
My father was vulnerable to chest infections.
Showing through his shirt, the layered felt
reeking of liniment was like the pelt
of some creature extinct in the Hebrides.
He refused to discard it until spring
brought the first buds to the trees.
Clearing out his things, I found a length
of the thick medicated wadding,
burying my face in its lasting strength.

Spring Ploughing

Restless metal roused me in the dawn,
chain-gang of ghosts going down again.
I opened the curtains. The stallion came
plodding from the home farm,
hooves big as dinner plates,
bobbing collar pear-shaped.
Archie led. His shins were lashed
with the hemp rope they used
to weigh down ricks in the wind.
Blinkered against diversion,
the horse waited at barred iron
while Archie staked, kneeling
to get the levels right.
The first furrow is always the hardest,
like the first bicycle on rutted mud,
first line without a ruler in school.
He held the long thin reins
like teasing kites into uncertain winds,
leaning back for the rise.
The earth turned like the black pages
of a tome discovered in an attic.
At dinner time Archie sat on the plough
and drank fresh frothing milk from a tin.
The horse had its nose in canvas.
Haloed by gulls, he ploughed again,
singing as wind plucked rusty wire,
either a love song or lullaby.
His shadow lengthened. When the sky
darkened and furrowed like the field
he unshackled the stallion,
led it towards the fire of the horizon.
Under the full moon, the black book
of the field shone.

The Jumping Field

With the light nights MacPhail would appear
over the hill, bare-footed, in shorts, Masai warrior
bringing news of a tribal victory, bamboo spear
in his fist a bar for our home-made stands
studded with squint nails. We'd lugged sand
in back-breaking sacks from the loch shore
for the long jump pit for the new sporting year.

The grainy film shot over half a century ago shows
MacPhail rolling over the bar into the sinking sun.
In the next frames you, Kenny, aged nine, run
through the tape held between our parents.
I am there too, a gangling boy vaulting
with the pliant sapling I cut with the Bushman.
Angus treads the sky in the hop step and jump.

MacPhail went back over the hill into the moon's circle,
taking the bamboo with him. He died in his prime,
and you, Kenny, are under turf in your own pit
that can't be turned over for the new season.
But when I rewind the fragile film
you rise from the sand, and MacPhail rolls up,
out of the sun, over the bar, to take it again.

Tradition Bearer

He was the last native speaker in the glen,
living in a cottage without power or sanitation,
and since there was no one with whom
to have a Gaelic conversation,
he spoke to the creatures in his native tongue
while he tossed them scraps, or hung
out the fat and peanuts of their winter fare.
He fed the fox and tended a tame hare.

He had no need of a wireless or a phone.
At night he sang love songs to the pipistrelles
that swayed on the rafters to his baritone,
and when he lit the lamp, saw his dead *màthair*
smiling in the chair she'd always occupied.
Scholars came to record his *sgeulachdan*,
only to discover, after he'd died,
that the tapes had nothing on them.

---

sgeulachdan: tales

The Last Monoglot Gaelic Speaker

I visited Peigi with my father in the 1960s.
He wanted, he said, to hear his native tongue
spoken without the corrupting influence of English.
She was ninety eight, had never been to the mainland.
Show her the picture of a train and she would have
reacted more through terror than curiosity.
She had been raised in an age of pumps and hooves.
We brought her salt herring in a Pyrex bowl,
but she would give us far more that afternoon,
eating the gift with her fingers as we spoke.

My father asked her about the supernatural.
One afternoon she had climbed Cnoc Fuar
and seen a fishing smack capsize in the calm,
the fathers of the crew not yet born.
'The skipper was a nephew of my son.
His body was carried out to the ocean.'
She masticated herring with the word *cuan*.
My father kissed the wispy skull as we left.
'The best Gaelic that I've ever heard,'
he said sadly as he latched her gate.

Potatoes

Big, snowy white, they
were ferried across

the choppy sound from Bonnavoulin,
ballast in the bottom of a skiff,
a native hand firm on the helm
turning into Tobermory.

Bonnavoulin. When he spoke,
it was as if the feast
were in his mouth,
served with the mackerel
trawled in their hundreds
off the light at Rudha nan Gall.

Balachan, native Gael, has gone.
Now potatoes are shipped in plastic,
frozen mackerel like fossils,
Gaelic on a compact disk.

Last Breath

I strike a match, whirl its flame
in the room in the infirmary
where my mother is dying.
This is what must be done
in the absence of the *dealan-dè*,
fire of God, the golden butterfly
that appears in the sick room
to escort the soul to the hereafter
through door or window
at the moment of death.

I hold the trembling flame
to her last breath.

Ceilidh

A high king in his wing chair
my father presided over the death of culture.

Visitors came, bearing gifts,
wrapped preciously in Gaelic.

All night the sea ran in the room,
rowers straining over the *iorram*.

Tormod, aged 60, sang of a young flame
and Finlay, the *Sgitheanach*, of shinty.

Father sipped his Islay Mist
listening to the lengthy *sgeulachd*.

Next morning, empty bottles, ashtrays,
a window open on the cleansing bay.

---

iorram: an oar-song
Sgitheanach: a person from the isle of Skye
sgeulachd: a tale

Elegy for *Fear Chanaidh*

John Lorne Campbell, Gaelic scholar, 1906-1996

It's not your mercury vapour lamp
burning at Sgor nam Ban Naomh tonight,
attracting moths to the flimsy trap.
At the scree the light is different,
as if the holy women are back in residence,
on their knees at their devotions,

the Norsemen having sailed home,
leaving their ruler at Uaigh Righ Lochlainn.
But your library is in darkness, though
every second morning you would go
to check the generator, to ensure
light would be shed on the day's page.

Seventy years since you heard island men
conversing in Gaelic at Oban Games
and became hopelessly infatuated.
In Barra there was no help for you.
'Abair siod fhathast, Iain' ('Say it again, John'),
the Coddy insisted, till you answered him.

In the house of Ruari Iain Bhain
the needle bit into the wax drum
as you recorded the Prince's welcome.
Among the floes of Alba Nuadh
Mrs Patterson of Benacadie
sang to you of Coire Bhreacain.

You died in Italy, among holy women
and butterflies drifting like blossom.
Tonight on Canna the unknown moth
beats its wings on the dark pane
where Dwelly's dictionary is shut,
a life of Gaelic complete.

Casting

Fished from bric-a-brac, not seen
for so many years, a fly box
the size of a wallet, dented tin.
I open it as if it is an icon.
Packed with gorgeous plumage,
looped casts like cherished locks.

Grandfather made them himself,
with steady hand by the Aladdin
dressing the barb with feathers
on nights of storm with the run
already turning into the estuary.
By morning his line would reach them.

This is a lost Gaelic dictionary.
I lay the big lure of bullock hair
and festive tinsel on my palm
to tempt *bradan* the salmon
in the peaty swirl. A small fly for the grilse,
'*òigh a' chuain*, virgin of the sea.

On June evenings in the meadow
he and my father fished for *bànagan*,
whispering in Gaelic as the lines
floated over their fly-festooned crowns,
the reel like the rasp of the *traon*
in the hayfield beneath the moon.

---

bànagan: sea trout
traon: corncrake

Flies like these are redundant now,
where the harsh reel pulls in
the spinning spoon.
There is one cast missing.
My father took it with him
when he turned for the ocean.

HMS *Sturdy*

In memory of Captain John Kennedy

You told me this story nearly fifty years ago
in the bar in Tobermory, on a winter's night
with the Atlantic running in the bay below
and the banshee shrieking in the chimney.
Home on leave on Tiree in autumn1940,
you had been walking on the western shore
when you became aware you were among
a group of five seamen.
'The hoods of their duffle coats were up,
and I could see against the setting sun
there was something wrong with their faces.
And I couldn't hear their seaboots on the shingle.'

Two days later, you were called out to assist
a destroyer that had run aground in a gale,
breaking in two off the west coast of Tiree.
Five men had tried to launch a rescue boat
but it had capsized in the heavy swell.
The five you had been walking with
on the western shore were the same men
you now helped to lift from the sea,
their faces blemished with salt,
seaboots filled with the ocean.
'They were making for their graves at Soroby,'
you added, trembling. 'Give me another whisky.'

Adapted from the Gaelic Notebooks
of Father Allan McDonald, Eriskay

I

While he was making the coffin
in a dark part of the dwelling
for the girl of feeble mind,
daughter of Angus of Garrynamonie,
with only a candle to guide him
Alex Steele the carpenter
said that he saw a lamb
surrounded by rays of light
standing in the box he had made.

He crossed himself with the blade
before fitting the lid.

II

'My daughter Flora saw him first,
at Abhainn 'ic Cuitheinn
when we were going home
in the early evening. The man
had his back towards us.
I couldn't see who it was.
He was wearing red braces
over his blue jersey.
We saw him wade into the sea
and dive under. We waited,
but he didn't reappear.
As you know, Father,
Flora was taken from me.'

III

Sailing at nightfall to Eriskay,
I asked the man:
'where on the shore
will we find our guide?'
'He won't be on the shore
but in his boat, Father.

The sea is holier
than the land.
Remember our Saviour
walking the sea at Galilee.
On board I keep holy water
close to hand.
I would not stay at night
upon the shore,
but on the sea
I have no fear,
even though
I have no light.'

IV

'That spring a bird with terrible scream
flitted across the island at night,
though it was never seen by day.
When it came to my dwelling
it seemed the door would break down
with the power of its wings
as I lay trembling in bed.
That autumn, many young people
died with measles on Eriskay,

among them my only daughter.
You will remember,
Maighstir Ailein:
you gave her the sacrament.'

V

'That night, rounding the Mull of Kintyre
I thought the smack was lost, Father.
I asked Donald to reef the sail
but the sea climbed aboard.
Then we saw the two men
standing on the foredeck,
wearing long Ulster coats.
They were talking in a strange tongue
and as Donald and I worked the sheets
they gave us their assistance.
In the calm of the morning
Donald said to me:
'Weren't these two men
your uncles who drowned
on a night such as the one
we have just come through?'

The Poet

At the end, laden with honours for his vision,
he knew less about the mysteries than the old woman
of my youth who subverted the theories of Einstein
by predicting when a healthy person would pass on,
even to the extent of seeing the date on the coffin.

Excursion

It's memory that greases the pistons.
Ever since the Broomielaw he's been watching
the engines, leaning on the railing.
The blurred paddle porthole is clearing
as the old *Waverley* beats into Rothesay
on the first Saturday of the Fair.
His father's searching the ship for him
while his mother waits at the gangway,
pressing her straw hat on her hair.
He has a room to himself at the Bay View
but he can't sleep. It's not the ozone
but the thought of clock golf, endless cones.
Those acrobatic cranks recall the pierrots when
a bob bought a lot of laughter in the Winter Gardens.

'The *Waverley* is now approaching Rothesay.'
He gets on his sticks, having put his bonnet on.
The engine sends a shudder through the spine
as he's helped up on deck before the gangway's gone.

Saithe

The faces in Francis Bacon portraits
always remind me of saithe,
blubber mouth and bulbous eyes,
mug of a mad pope. Cats
wouldn't touch those fish
we hauled with bamboos
and baited hooks
from the black rock by Connel Bridge.

The mussel, a miser's purse,
hard to prise open,
green stuff inside

wound round the hook,
tied on with thread.

To haul up saithe
is a waking nightmare.
First dirty silver
striped and forked,
the half-seen skull
breaking the tide-race,
then finally,
the gasping face.

On Cat Bells

His father's his sherpa.
Aged in months
he rides the backpack frame,
urging his carrier
up the tricky terrain,
snow on Fools' morning.

Coleridge scaling Helvellyn
higher on moonshine than laudanum
was never as happy as this bonneted baby
reaching for the mobile
of ducks over Derwentwater.

His bare heels urge his bearer
as the sky tilts,
the track beginning to tell
on new trainers.
He shakes his rattle
like a lama's prayer-bell.

Foreign Correspondent

He built his career on atrocity. He was there
when Belsen was liberated, and ad-libbed
a moving account for the newsreel
as bulldozers shifted the corpses behind him.
He reported to you from Kenya
when the Mau Mau were hacking the white man
to death. He was with the Yanks in Vietnam,
and described the child, alight with napalm,
fleeing from the low-flying plane,
for which he received a commendation.

Too frail to go to Iraq, nevertheless
he's wheeled out on our screen nightly
to comment on footage of the car bombs.
'It will get worse before it gets better.'
His face is lined, grim looking
as if all the awfulness he's seen
has sunk into his pores.
He lives on the adrenalin of death,
reminiscing about wars and catastrophe.

Bonspiel

He saw the weather written on the pane
as he buckled on his gaiters,
shouldering the hammer to walk the lane
spooked with his breath, to the pond
at the extremity of his acres.
The hammer bounced on the ice
a dozen times before he was certain
that it would bear the weight.
He took the pungent moth-balls
from the pockets of his plus-fours
before sending the serving-man
with a message round the doors:
'Bonspiel at Murdo's pond, tomorrow, noon.'

They came on foot, on horseback, by trap,
ladies in breeches, ploughmen with twine
lashing their shins for the only game
in the district. The shelves in the brick shed
were lined with stones like ancient cheeses,
each one owned by a chalked name.
Men down on a knee, as if proposing,
send the stone slithering across the ice,
its way hastened by scrabbling brooms.
Stones clash, and by the pond's edge
a brazier offers searing chestnuts.

The pond has leached into the earth now,
reverting to a bog. In the bracken
I uncover the brazier's rusted remains,
like a cauldron from an abandoned coven.

The door of the shed hangs off its hinges.
I lift down a stone from the dusty shelves,
the granite cracked from the collision
in the forgotten bonspiel. As I send it
spinning across the floor I hear
the roar, and through the broken window
see a beauty brushing up her game.

Katherine Mansfield at Fontainebleau

The Master built me a couch above the cows
so that their sweet breath
would help my lungs. As for death,
I want to get the dying over
so that I can be reborn.
I drink frothing milk from the pail.
Gurdjieff presides in the study-house
on his raised dais
with carpets from Baluchistan,
watching the Dalcroze dance.
The word melts like marzipan
in my mouth. I cough again:
I spent a morning in the forge,
watching our bald-headed Titan
hammering the iron.
'Work in this place
is an end and not a means.'
I cut my hair in a fringe
because Murry is coming.
Should we move south
in search of the sun?
'Balance the centre,' The Master says.
The cows are lowing,
life pouring red from my mouth.

Kiloran, Colonsay

The sand shifted. An iron rivet
still gripping timber. Many more.
The next find, four bronze buttons
carried in a cap to the big house.
Sir Malcolm himself ordered them

to dig with their hands.
Sand sifted from the cranium.
Now, scales with a balance beam,
by a broken sword.
'They tipped the boat over him.'

Vikings: merchants of death,
wading ashore on Iona.
Blathmac wouldn't confess
where the saint's shrine was buried.
They cut short the conventual Mass.

'Dig on, there may be more,'
urged Sir Malcolm, ordering
a ring of lanterns in the sand.
'Move out on your knees, men,
so as to miss nothing.'

Nearby, they uncovered the horse,
legs drawn up, neck
stretched to the north. Sir Malcolm
noted the right hind-limb:
the metatarsal bone cut clean.

And then a spade struck a slab.
While a man went for a lantern
Sir Malcolm knelt in the sand,
tracing the braille of the incision.
'This is definitely Christian.'

He gave each man a sovereign.
The butler carried the finds
up on a tray to the mansion where
Sir Malcolm labelled them
with his gold Waterman.

The sand shifts again. Today
at Kiloran the glittering jewel
turns into the ring-pull
from a can. Next, a notched stick.
Nearby, a dead dog in black plastic.

Shearwaters, the Treshnish Isles

In the dwelling beside our bivouac
the window to the west has fallen.
Is this what has allowed the *slaugh*,
host of the dead, to come in
at nightfall? We hear their eerie cry,
kitty-coo-roo, *kitty-coo-roo*,
as if they're lamenting the ruin
that was once their habitation
before the failure of the potato
in the terrible famine.

They spend daylight out at sea,
returning at night
to the ruins on Lunga.
In the beam of our light
they blunder about the sky,
clumsy trapeze artistes,
colliding, falling, soaring,
before swooping to the burrow
to feed their offspring.
They will be gone by dawn.

Wheatears

Adapted from *Carmina Gadelica*

A peat under an arm, the scholars found
the dry stone wall tumbled in the coldest spell
in living memory, and frozen balls
beaked and feathered strewn on the ground.
Heedless of the clanging hand-bell,
though that could mean a thrashing,
they scooped them into their balmorals,
laying them in front of the schoolroom fire
on which they'd heaped their own offering.
One maiden even unbuttoned her dress,
placing the frozen ball between breasts
that would not bud till the coming spring.
After the geography lesson the *clacharan*
began to flutter, then one flew round the room,
beating against the globe, as if indicating
it should be in Africa, instead of hibernating
in a wall on Islay. They came from all over the island
to witness the miracle, small birds brought back
from the dead, perching on the hand,
accepting crumbs of cheese, wintering
in Bailemeadhonach instead of Basutoland.

Ptarmigan Mating

On top of the world
for the white wedding of the year.
3000 feet up on Cruachan
he is dressed like Elton John,
wattles rose-coloured spectacles.

In this camouflage of camouflages
he displays a dandy black tail.
She purrs in appreciation.

Her voice is like
a champagne cork
being turned slowly.

Rock sparkles like glass
as she froths towards him.

At Mugdock Reservoir

For my brother

Heel reflectors catch the sunset
as joggers pound round the reservoir,
and you, Kenny, who were always the loner,
are back with the evening star.

You've come a long way
since that evening in late May
you ran this path as the sun went down,
trainers pounding the tarmac.

Dearest brother, as you lap me
I see you are leaner, fitter, now,
eyes fixed on the way ahead,
but no footfall, no burst of breath.

Destination

Overnight at Christmas the train arrived: red tin,
with the passengers painted on the carriages.
I slotted in the rails, wound the mechanism
and in the dawn the train began its run
looping under the legs of chairs, back again,
and then under a bridge – an aunt's present –
then through a station where the master stood,
a red flag under his oxter. Through a wood
planted only in the imagination.
I rewound it with the silver key,
feeling the tightening of the spring.

Now Christmases are measured in diminishing tracks:
no longer the figures of eight stretching
over the floor, passing the painted herd
staring over a realistic gate, finishing
with the long run across the carpet.
I have difficultly slotting the rails together,
knowing they can't run in loops any more,
under the sideboard and out of the door.
They don't even go in a circle now,
but in a straight line. The signal's
up, red flag raised, but before
the mechanism runs out, the rails will.

Iona

Monks with stained fingers from the bestiary
took their meals, *alfresco*,
at this slab left by the glacier
above the sound of Iona
as they conversed in Irish.
Danes sometimes dropped in.

A thousand years on, chisels
inserted into the seams split the stone.
Men bowed their heads
under the blessed lintel
as they entered the home
where the lamp from the sea burned.

I bow my head as I enter
the restored building that sells
reproductions of the Book of Kells.
They took it to Ireland for safety,
but the slab was too heavy.

Annals of Iona

In memory of Alisdair Dougal, David Kirkpatrick,
Logie MacFadyen, Robert Hay. † 13 December 1998

AD 749. 'The drowning of the family of Iona.'
So the Irish annalist records with brevity.
Was it the entire monastery,
under the sail's broken wing,
in the sound or open ocean?

Christ is our helmsman:
he will not turn from the storm
even if it means white martyrdom
on the rocks of Torran.

Brethren from Daire Columcille
will arrive on the next tide
to till the ground
and say Mass for the drowned.

The porpoise rolls in the swell
and off Torran, the petrel
dances on the wall of the breaker
gathering for the kill.

A few hours before matins
an outboard engine begins.
No light in the monastery
to guide those at sea.

Who will sow the harvest
and raise the creels from the reef
after this wave has run north,
leaving its wash of grief?

Across the dark sound
we do not know if there is another shore,
a cliff to climb,
a light under a door.

Aes Fors, Mull

First the Celts: seen from the coracle
out of Iona, vertical water.
For the Vikings, a mare's tail
of spume from the longship
holding their blades in the wake
after the slaughter
of the monastery,
holy vessels chiming in the stern.

Two languages running together
from the hillside, dropping
as intertwined water.
Not that waterfalls need naming:
long after man
they will be cascading,
splashing, seeking the sea.

The Fisherman

He has been seen in plus-fours and two-way hat
on the avenue at Bonawe House, carrying a rod,
fingers locked through the gills of the salmon
he took from Poll Fearn, the Alder Tree Pool.
The evening he walks in was before the artillery
of the blitzkrieg recoiled in the lanes of Poland.
The fragrance of his pipe mingles with blossom
as he goes home at sunset, carrying his supper
through a landscape of Gaelic names.
The fall of his brogue never scared the otter,
nor did he cast his shadow on the water.
He has no shadow tonight among shadowy trees.

Dolphins off Mull

Tonight at Calgary Bay
the sea boils with dolphins.
Leumadair, the leaper;
maybe a score of them,
backs breaking water
as they rise
steeper and steeper
until it seems
they might disappear
into the skies.

They accompanied the coracle
that brought the saint to Iona,
with gospels in waterproof skins.
They lay offshore
when Vikings struck
when the monks were at matins.
They rode the wash
of the invasion ships for North Africa,
pensive soldiers at the rail
watching their phosphorescence.

When I am a shade
standing on Cnoc Udmail
will dolphins still be here,
cavorting in the swell,
or will the pod be stranded,
radar damaged by pollution,
beached on Calgary Sands,
all joy and energy gone,
eyes heavy with recrimination,
dying in the sinking sun?

Girl with Mobile Phone

She sits in the Gardens, gazing
into the small lighted window
of her mobile phone,
finger on the button.
How will the call come,
text or spoken, saying:

'I Luv U. See U @ 8?'
Not now, though this is
the cheap time. The gate
will close in half an hour.
She presses the keys
in her desperation,

sending out the signal:
an ordinary girl in Glasgow,
on a summer evening
in the Botanics
wishes to hear from you.

A Snowball in Summer

He bounds down Meall Riaghain,
outdistancing the stag
in the summer dawn,
no time to admire the prospect
across Loch Etive, to Trilleachan
where glacial stones ring
with the oystercatcher's tune,
and at Ard Uisneachan
Naoise and Deirdre are home
in the 'cattlefold of the sun.'

Less than an hour to pay his due,
the snowball from the corrie
wrapped in his plaid,
next to his racing heart,
down past the glade
hazed by the charcoal mounds,
gasping as he rolls
the melting sphere
on the table of the factor,
in Glen Noe to collect the rent

from the Macintyres,
a snowball in summer from Cruachan
ticked off on the ledger,
before he rides to Taymouth
to tell Breadalbane,
laughing over a glass of wine
at the charming custom
of the sons of the carpenter,

his trusted swordsmen,
settling their dues in snow.

A rent we could no longer pay,
even if we still tenanted Glen Noe,
because the summer snow
is disappearing from Coire Chat
and soon in winter also
the whiteness will be gone
from Drochaid Glas.
A key turned in Porto Rico
is melting the glacier
and ruining our clan history.

To a Child

This is now your inheritance:
first the scorching sun,
now the monsoon in hemispheres
where it never blew.
I bequeath to you
the river devoid of fish,
the bush empty of song.
It is my wish
that you accept with good grace,
without rancour or blame.
Mistakes can happen.

The Natural World

Waddling across the floe, the penguin heard the creak
of the glacier on the move after an age. Its beak
tested the thinning ice under which it could see
the walrus swimming, searching. But the sea
was devoid of fish, devoid of the blue whale,
giant of the deep, hoovering up the krill.
The penguin saw no point in the migration
to its breeding ground, where, instead of snow,
the sun would beat down on the huddled colony.
The last sea lion had drowned, the last seal
slithered from the ice, the last albatross
crash-landed on the melting runway.
The Antarctic's melting is all our loss,
not just creatures that have had their day.

Ben Dorain, 2030

You, Macintyre kinsman,
were able to wax lyrical
about the deer on Ben Dorain.
Acid rain has eaten the lichen
and the corries are lacking snow.
The walker listens in vain
for the stags' rutting roar
and watches in vain for
the arrow of the peregrine
streaking down the glen.

It is no longer possible
to be inspired by a mountain
that has sustained such damage
through pollution.
The resonant Gaelic names
that the bard delighted in,
such as *fraigh* Choire-Chruiteir,
Harper's Corrie scarp, have gone
with the light-rumped herd
that mated there.

Woodland Burial

I sign the paper for the woodland burial,
two graves side by side, cardboard coffins,
a planted tree part of the bargain.
No headstone, no pretentious inscription,
nothing to identify our resting place
or that we have ever been on earth.
No ear-muffed sexton on a ride-on mower,
autumn leaves dispersed by a blower,
flowers rotting in the sunken vase.
Our bodies will nourish the canopy,
in time our arms support a bough
on which a mistle thrush will sing.
This is our contribution to global warming,
to the anonymity that death should be.
You may walk across our graves
without fear of the old superstition,
make love against the trunk
that has absorbed the nutrition
of our bodies.
It's called resurrection.

Planting

With every book
should come a seedling
to replace the tree they took
from the forest
so that you may have
the wisdom of the word.
Water it faithfully
so that it grows
into a mighty canopy
that will give you more pleasure
than an entire library.

Lament for the *Cuach*

I have been listening at Coille Chronan,
the singing wood, for a fortnight now,
but still the cuckoo has not come,
the first year in living memory.
I was in my cradle at the door
when I first heard it calling.
It was vocal in the glen
as if there were a dozen of them
when I was cutting peats on the hill.
I heard it on the night of my nuptials.
It came to me in Italy
in the valley below the monastery,
and its crossing of the Rapido
was my last sight of the world
before I stood on the mine.

The wood is without song and foliage.
I walked up there this morning,
guided by the clever dog
that used to muster my flock,
feeling my way along the fank wall,
the bitter rain on my lips,
the lichen dead under my touch.
Though I stand here for the whole spring
the *cuach* will not call.

Christmas Future

Lubricated with resin, the Bushman's blade
sang through the symmetrical tree we had chosen
against the moon. Our breaths made
spectres in the plantation as the pine fell,
putting roosting pigeons to flight. Our frozen
hands dragged the lopped top clear.
Within the hour its branches were hung with bells
of silver, a fairy at the top where a bird had sung.

The Bushman is rusting on the wall.
In the Christmases to come, no more trees
because of global warming.
The eastern star's dimmed by the man-made haze,
the gift of frankincense a scarce resource.
Cut a tree for Christmas and the world, its breath
already laboured, is close to death.

Climate Change

Somewhere in Africa
a man fishing termites
with a peeled stick
will have noticed the nights,
colder now,
the haze from Nairobi
like a new nebula.
One morning he will wake
to a film of ice
on his lips.

Habitations

Our fathers built in stone and Gaelic:
plumb-line laid along
the block of Ross of Mull granite,
limestone bonded with a song.

Habitations built to last,
four-square against the Atlantic blast.
Gaelic raised the roof
of Belnahua slates.

Houses come by ferry now,
walls made of shavings and glue,
erected in a day or two,
double glazing to exclude the sea.

Mowing in Winter

A month before Christmas and he's cutting grass.
The mower he rides on belches dioxide.
How has this seasonal shift come to pass?
Above, an aeroplane takes a joyride,
leaving the tainted breath of its trail.
What have we done to the world, I ask
as he starts the next machine? His next task's
blowing the autumn leaves from A to B,
though winds will blow them back again.
His house needs heated these winter nights,
the thermostat already up to maximum.
'I cannot sleep without a light,'
he tells me as he fills the chain-saw.
I tell him we have an obligation
to conserve on energy.
'It will see out my time,' he says.
'Let the next generation do the worrying.'

The Best Years

We had the best of it; Rock and Roll; Woodstock;
John and Yoko in their Amsterdam love-in.
From now on it's downhill, dry run to oblivion.
The chair-lift's rusting, and when did you last
hear the cuckoo in the glen? The clock's
no longer ticking. Instead the drip drip
of the glacier, the sea under the foundations,
the latest laptop thrown into a skip.
We had the best of it: let those to come
clear up the mess if they can.

Decrofted

This was Archie's croft. In the spring
as he ploughed peewits cuffed him
for planting on their territory.
The fence sagged where he leaned
on golden evenings, talking Gaelic
with my father.

Today a drum revolves, spewing
concrete all over his acreage,
Sold to a couple from the south.
Next week the ferry brings their kit house,
double glazing and a garage
where peewits parked on their eggs.

Late News

After the surprise eviction
From the Big Brother House, an item
at the tail-end of the bulletin.
Because the Pole is melting,
bears are swimming
up to 60 miles, searching for floes
to fish from. The clip shows
a carcass like a sodden white rug
bobbing in the ocean.

'Tune in at eleven for the latest
news from the Big Brother House
to find who may be next.'

Dementia

I was nine when I had pneumonia: you slept with me
in the room with the bell-tower at Dunstaffnage,
trying to draw the fever into your own body.
In the lamp-light the lance of the thermometer
withdrawn from my oxter reached 103.
'I thought that night that I had lost you,
you were so hot, so delirious.'
I began to scream, seeing the menagerie
come lumbering through the wall,
grotesque creatures, a unicorn with fire for horn.
The horse-hair mattress was soaked through.
When I was recovering you took my hand
down the avenue. I had to relearn the world again
– that there was no menace even in a hen.

Fifty years on, I hear you as I approach the portico,
the glass door engraved with a full-sailed galleon
beating towards the Clyde with a full cargo,
because this was the mansion of a tobacco baron,
now a nursing home. But no narcotic
can soothe you tonight as you flail about
in your wheelchair, screaming, lashing out,
rounding on me. 'Oh you're here, you bastard.
Why have you put me in this bloody place?'
Because you are no longer the person
you once were when you lay with me
in that room at Dunstaffnage: your brain,
the scan shows, is cratered like the moon,
your personality changed beyond recognition.

Out for an evening stroll in his walled garden
at Dunstaffnage in the '30s, Angus Campbell
saw you in the distance, sampling a rose bush,
and mistook you for Lady Masserene, the Irish beauty.
I have a faded photo of you, by the wishing stone,
in ankle-length dress and floppy hat, the fashion model.
You had several suitors, but finally settled on
the Gaelic poet roaring up the avenue on his Norton.
After hair-raising bends you found white heather
in your shoes. Four sons: in polka-dot dress and straw-hat
you led your brood down to Loch Etive, rubbing lotions
on our skin against the burning sun, bottles of lemonade
laid in the tidal shallows to cool. Dress hitched, you wade
as we become flippered frogmen scuttling *Prinz Eugen*.

I no longer act like a cross-dresser in Lingerie,
skulking among the rails. Instead I carry
my basket of purchases to the check-out,
the flickering scanner dragged over the price-tags.
Size 10 slacks, tights, cotton panties – three carrier bags.
Crossing to Boots, I present your Advantage Card
to keep your name alive, though I have legal control
over bank account, life – everything except your soul.
I kneel to fit the dinky slippers that close with Velcro.
Once a week a woman comes in to set your hair,
about which you were always so particular,
sitting under the heated hood in the Tobermory salon.
Its whiteness has the soft texture of cashmere
as it falls through my fingers in the nursing home.

Burns Night, a supper in the hall, the residents
arranged at the long board in their best clothes.
No Immortal Memory, Toast to the Lassies.
(How could the bard have understood old age,
far less the terror of the tattered mind?)
Most of them are demented, some almost blind.
They scatter haggis, slurp juice from plastic glasses.
A man with a keyboard sings *A Red Red Rose*.
I see you smiling, as if you're in repose
at the top table at a Burns Supper on Mull,
in evening dress and jewellery, while
your eloquent husband extols the bard's genius.
Then Bobby straps on his accordion
and plays *A Red Red Rose* for you.

After a night of violence and insults, I demand
to see a psychiatrist as soon as possible.
'Your mother has been taken off Mellaril,
the anti-psychotic drug, because it's suspected
of causing fatal heart rhythms in certain cases,
and is being withdrawn for use in dementia.'
'But nothing else works,' I argue. 'Without this pill
she's a demon, striking out at the staff, me, you, anyone.
Don't you think it would be kinder if her heart gave way,
even through a prohibited drug like Mellaril
than having to endure the terror, the indignity
of not knowing who she is, was, or where she is?
I'd rather see her at peace than this hellish humiliation.'
'I understand,' he says, renewing the prescription.

The *King George* went to the breakers' yard years ago,
but we're sailing on her down the Sound of Mull
in the heat-haze, homeward bound for Tobermory.
I'm a teenager again, sitting across from you in the saloon
of spotless napery, stewards in white tunics, silver cutlery.
Framed by the panoramic window, like a Sergent portrait,
your looks turn the heads of diners. 'There's Colonel
Robertson, a great friend of your father. Hullo!'
Mother, you're waving to a man dead for thirty years.
Besides, father hated him. I want to disembark
and be my proper age, but matron is firm:
'Best to go along with her, otherwise she'll have a tantrum.'
Always the dutiful son, I call 'Hullo' to Colonel Robertson.
This steamer will never reach its destination.
We are caught in a time-warp of your creation.

Feeding time: sight ruined by macular degeneration,
you bend your weary old face to the plate, a fish finger,
half a dozen fries, more like a meal for a nursery.
I fork in the food, wiping your mouth with the napkin.
You suck the cup with plastic teat, milk dribbling,
as you suckled me in infancy. I am the parent
of an eighty year old hanging in straps from her chair
as I hung from the high-chair in the war years of scarcity.
Tonight I've brought you a treat, a tub of ice cream.
When it's finished you lick the spoon.
Your bones are bound together with blue veins,
your utterances like a child learning language
when, like an eclipse, the occlusion
passes over the dark side of your brain.

I danced the Highland Fling in trews for the Xmas party.
A few nights later, as I came in a man popped up
from behind a chair and saluted me. 'Evening, Colonel.
I've got the squad ready for a raid.' He points across
to a potted plant. 'The Japs are hiding in these trees.'
They call him Wee Eck: with the Royal Scots
in Singapore in '41, he earned a commendation
for refusing to surrender. The bow-legged conquerer
unsheathed his blade, but instead of beheading him,
beat him until he was nearly dead, sending him to spend
five years in Changi, eating rat shit among rice sweepings.
'Carry on, sergeant,' I instruct him, but I am weeping,
because any of us can go this way, the brain's
black holes into which memories have fallen.

When you wet yourself, you're wheeled away.
From the bathroom I hear the machine
like a coffee grinder pulping the sodden nappy.
You were always so fastidious: the neat bow
at your blouse, the lights strung on the tree
in the tower alcove when we came home
for Christmas; the Watchnight Service,
beds turned down, the colossal turkey,
the pudding studded with silver sixpences.
For ceilidhs I helped you fold the tickets
for the tombola wheel, the majority
of them apologising: 'sorry no luck.'
You drew a dud ticket in life's lottery,
after a lifetime's unselfish service.

After so many visits they think I'm one of them, handing out
the cake, separating the fights, alerting assistants
when one of them needs the toilet. I've seen piss trickling
from the chair, the tear trickling from the clouded eye.
In their exhausted faces I've seen the wish to die
incapable of articulation since they've mislaid
their language with their knitting and the sports section.
Some of them don't even know their own names.
There are those with no visitors, no relatives. They sit
staring at the television screen, unsmiling at the comedian,
Les Dawson as the elderly woman mouthing his coy messages
about things not spoken of, female problems.
Sometimes they shout out a name. No one pays attention.

You see that woman, head bowed between her thighs?
She was one of the finest painters of her generation,
her work in galleries, including the Tate Modern.
She noticed she wasn't painting what her eyes
were seeing, as if she'd reverted to Impressionism.
When she signed her name, it was someone else's she wrote.
Now she sits mute in the corner all day, the palette
of her mind scrambled. She's now colour-blind,
her sense of perspective gone, along with inspiration.
It must be like living in a world of cubism,
where a limb is where it shouldn't be, an eye
in the centre of a forehead. But she won't die
because though the mind has gone, the body's strong.
She will have to live with her fearful vision.

Every night the Irishman meets me at the door:
'what goes up but never comes down again?'
It's safer to shake my head in ignorance.
'Your age!' he roars. When he's being beaten
at draughts he brings his metal stick crashing
down on the board, scattering the pieces.
Heather appears on the landing with two cases,
a beaming smile. She's going home. Descending,
the catches splay, bras and panties tumbling.
In her frustration she punches me. One evening
of rare lucidity she shows me photos
of her happy family before dementia kicked in at sixty.
She's moving to a mental ward, luggage sent in advance,
and will no longer recognise her next of kin.

Some evenings it's calm and pleasant, like the old days
in our island home, with you sitting at the window
overlooking the bay, reminiscing about your life
in London. Resting in bed, you nod and smile
as if miraculously your brain has repaired itself,
your memory restored, the tantrums gone.
Except that, round me, the apparatus of frailty.
In the bathroom the hoist like a guillotine.
Through in the lounge, the air-filled chair
I bought to ease the racking pain of your skeleton.
I know that tonight's lucidity is only temporary.
Make the most of it. I tell you a story
about these happy days in Tobermory
until you fall asleep, clutching my hand.

At 2a.m. the phone rings. 'Your mother's dying.
You'd better come right away.' The roads are quiet
at this ungodly hour, a scavenging vixen easing
out through the bars of the Botanic Gardens,
a clubber tottering home, carrying her shoes.
You no longer seem to be breathing.
'She'll be gone soon,' matron assures me,
as we sit on either side of your bed,
each holding a hand as your face turns blue.
But before the dawn chorus from the patio
you're sitting up, sipping a cup of tea
and by lunch-time you are raging.
I have had several of these false alarms
and get angry with this resurrection.
It would have been release for both of us.

The consultant sends for me. 'We'll have to stop
feeding your mother. Her food's going into her lungs.
'Don't worry, she'll be gone in a week, peacefully.'
You lasted longer, in hospital, a drip under the skin
to keep your body cool and moistened.
Your beauty begins to fade, your face assumes
the hewn features of an Easter Island effigy.
Day and night your sons keep vigil by your bed.
On my watch I re-read much of Tolstoy, the smell
of death as distinct as Borodino. You passed away
on Armistice Sunday, when I was at church,
praying for you. By the time I got back,
they were hassling my brother about moving the body,
the bed needed for another casualty.

Tobermory Days
stories from an island

Lorn Macintyre

ISBN: 1 902831 56 X   224 pages   £7.99 pbk

Archie Maclean is the bank manager, enthu-
siast for the Gaelic and inveterate hobbyist –
he points his cine camera at life on Main
Street. Just as this collection of stories does,
his lens captures the range and depth of the
lives of people under a fast-changing and
fast-fading West Highland cloud.

Gille Ruadh, the red (haired) boy, is the son of
the telephonist in the island's manual ex-
change, and is Maclean's connecting rod to
the hub of local life. It conducts a powerful
and insightful charge – strong in humour,
love, tragedy, pain and darkness.

Evoking the storytelling and reflective gifts of
Iain Crichton Smith or Robin Jenkins,
Lorn Macintyre has created a brilliantly
incisive and entertaining collection rooted in
his own Hebridean background.

●

Tobermory Tales
stories from an island

Lorn Macintyre

ISBN: 1 902831 78 0   224pages   £7.99 paperback

In this sequel to **Tobermory Days**, Lorn Macintyre's hugely acclaimed first collection of stories, the author continues to capture the essence of life in the Hebridean Islands. His writing touches the lives of the people of the island of Mull, both native Gael and aspirational incomer. Neither romantic nor overly realist, Macintyre has a lightness of touch that produces stories that are hugely entertaining and moving.

'vivid and graceful. . . an excellent short story collection'
The Herald

'vibrant and vivid'   **Sunday Herald**

'a beautifully realised piece of fiction. . .
with compelling and exhilarating style'
West Highland Free Press

'humour mingles with tragedy. . . enjoy the quality of the writing,
savour it story by story'   **Scots Magazine**

●